SAN AUGUSTINE PUBLIC LIBRARY

	DATE DUE		

SAN AUGUSTINE PUBLIC LIBRARY

TO RENEW THIS BOOK
CALL 275-5367

REACHING FOR THE STARS

SELENA
The Queen of Tejano

Jill C. Wheeler

Published by Abdo & Daughters, 4940 Viking Drive, Suite 622, Edina, Minnesota 55435.

Printed in the United States.

Cover Photo credit: Archive Photos
Interior Photo credits: Wide World Photos, pages 7, 15, 21, 26, 29
Archive Photos, pages 5, 11, 18, 24, 31

Edited by Julie Berg

Wheeler, Jill C., 1964
    Selena, The Queen of Tejano / Jill C. Wheeler.
        p.   cm.
Summary: Examines the life and work of the award-winning Texas singer who had begun to popularize Tejano music when she was shot and killed.
ISBN 1-56239-523-8
1. Selena, 1971-1995—Juvenile literature. 2. Tejano musicians Biography—Juvenile literature. [1. Selena, 1971-1995. 2. Singers. 3. Mexican Americans—Biography. 4. Tejano music.] I. Title.
ML3930.S43W54   1995
782.42164—dc20
[B]   95-30175
                                             CIP
                                            AC MN

TABLE OF CONTENTS

SING A SONG OF TEXAS

There's a special sound in the Rio Grande region of Texas and Mexico. It's a type of music called Tejano (tay-HA-no). Tejano reflects many cultures — just like the people who live in the Rio Grande Valley. It is a mixture of polka, Mexican, Latin, popular, country, rap and blues music.

Tejano is bouncy and upbeat. The music has been a favorite in the Rio Grande for many years. It dates back almost 100 years to the first Mexican Americans in the region. In fact, Tejano musicians still sing their songs in Spanish. On any night, you can find brightly dressed couples whirling to Tejano music on the dance floor.

Few people outside of Texas and Mexico know about Tejano. For many years, Tejano fans thought their music would remain a secret to most people.

Then came one very special musician. She was a Tejano singer with beauty, charm and a soaring soprano voice. Her name was Selena Quintanilla Perez (suh-LEE-nuh kin-tah-KNEE-yah pear-EZ). Most people called her Selena.

Selena Quintanilla Perez, the queen of Tejano music.

At age 23, Selena already had won two Grammy Awards. Her records had sold millions of copies. She had received six Tejano Music Awards, and was a role model for thousands of Hispanic young people. She had also won a part in a new movie. It was clear Selena was going to be a star. Selena would introduce the world to Tejano.

Tragically, Selena's promising career ended with a single gun shot. Yet her life story still carries a message of hope as bright as her music.

A FAMILY OF MUSICIANS

Selena was born on April 16, 1971, in Lake Jackson, Texas. Her father, Abraham Quintanilla Jr., had moved the family to Lake Jackson to work for a chemical company. Yet he didn't want to be there. His roots were in Corpus Christi, Texas. He had been a musician before taking his new job. Abraham wanted to be a musician once again.

Abraham Quintanilla Jr., father of Selena Quintanilla Perez.

So did Selena. She sang in public when she was six years old. When she was seven, Abraham knew his daughter would be a professional singer. He soundproofed the family's garage and formed a band. He taught his son, Abraham III, called A.B., to play the guitar. He taught his other daughter, Suzette, to play the drums. He asked Selena to sing. Selena's mother, Marcella, encouraged the new band and traveled with them.

The band played at family gatherings. By 1979, the Quintanillas added two more members and gave the band a name — "Los Dinos" ("The Guys").

Now, Los Dinos was ready to play for pay. Selena's father became the band's business manager. He booked the band at weddings and parties. They also played most weekends at Abraham's new Mexican restaurant. People started talking about Los Dinos. They loved to dance to their music.

In 1982, Abraham had to close his restaurant. The price of oil had dropped so much, many oil workers lost their jobs. Abraham's restaurant did not have enough business to stay open.

Now, Los Dinos had to earn money to support the family. Selena recalled those days. "We were literally doing it to put food on the table," she said. Abraham decided to give his family's music special attention. They moved back to Corpus Christi and Los Dinos cut a record.

'Selena was only nine years old when she and Los Dinos recorded an album at a studio in Houston, Texas. The record was not popular right away. Yet little by little, Spanish radio stations began playing the songs. The disk jockeys who worked at the stations were very fond of Selena's music. In 1983, they gave her an award. They called it the Mocking Bird Award.

Few people had ever heard of the Mocking Bird Award. It made them curious. They wanted to hear more from this young woman who sang so beautifully. More people asked Los Dinos to play for them.

Selena's first break came when she was just fifteen years old. She won two categories in the Tejano Music Awards. Judges named her best female vocalist and performer of the year.

LIFE ON THE ROAD

Selena had an unusual childhood. She spent many hours traveling to gigs where the band would play. Her life was not all business, however. She was the clown of the family. She loved to play hide-and-seek, and eat double pepperoni pizza. She was a natural athlete who could run as well as she could sing.

Selena had dreams of her own, too. She loved to draw, especially clothing. She hoped one day to design clothing. She was hard-working, and helped support her family with her singing. She also sold candy and fancy pencils to her classmates to earn extra money.

Selena attended West Oso Junior High School in Corpus Christi. There, she excelled at art and physical education. "She always wanted to be the best, and she was the best," said one of her teachers.

When Selena entered high school, she chose a different path. She couldn't go to classes like most students. Her work with the band kept her on the road.

The Cathedral in Corpus Christi, Texas, the city Selena called home.

Instead, she signed up for a correspondence course. She earned her high school degree while keeping her music career in full swing.

Selena's years of traveling, performing and hard work paid off in 1989. Her band, now called "Selena y Los Dinos" ("Selena and the Guys"), signed a contract with the record company EMI. The following year, one of Selena's fans, Yolanda Saldivar, saw the singer in concert in San Antonio. Yolanda started a Selena Fan Club. The club grew to 9,000 members in just four years.

When Selena and Los Dinos signed with EMI, the band still included Selena's older brother, A.B., and her older sister, Suzette. It also had a new man — Chris Perez. Chris played the bass guitar.

Selena and Chris became good friends. Chris liked the way Selena could express her feelings. He found her fun-loving. By 1991, he realized his feelings for her went beyond friendship. So did Selena. The two were married on April 2, 1992.

Even as a newlywed, Selena could look back on a string of successes. People now called her Tejano's biggest star. Her album "Ven Conmigo" ("Come With Me") went gold in 1991. It also made her the first female Tejano recording artist to score a Gold Record. No one doubted that Selena's star was rising.

HITTING THE BIG-TIME

In 1993, EMI released a collection of the band's songs called "Selena Live!" The album captured the excitement Selena created whenever she was on stage. She had a way of captivating an audience. She wore flashy costumes that earned her comparisons with other famous stars.

"I don't like to compare artists, but Selena is the closest artist I've got to Madonna," said an EMI executive. "She has that same control. I love artists that know where they want to go and how to get there. She's definitely a pop star."

In November 1993, Selena signed an international recording contract with SBK Records. SBK is a sister company of EMI.

SBK produces records in English. It was an exciting move for Selena and her band. Now they would get a chance to cross over into American pop music.

"I hope we're able to expand in a different (musical direction)," Selena told reporters after she signed the record deal. "This market is a whole new ballpark for us."

SBK executives also were excited. "I had never even heard of Tejano music before," said the SBK vice president who signed Selena. "But I was just so impressed seeing this girl up there on stage. I think she has every element for international success. An amazing voice, a phenomenal stage presence, gorgeous looks, and a great personality."

Yet among Selena's fans, the announcement created mixed feelings. Some were excited that Selena was taking the next step in her career. Other Tejano fans were afraid they would lose their star. Selena tried to calm their fears. "Just because we signed a contract with an English company doesn't mean we're going to leave our base," she said. "I think a lot of

Selena moving into the big time.

people who have supported us would be very disappointed if we were to turn our backs and go on to something else."

FAMILY FIRST

Selena also reassured her fans that her new career wouldn't change her values. "Family comes first," she said. "It always will."

Despite her success, Selena never forgot how important her family was in her life. She maintained a private life very different from her personality on the stage. Offstage, she was family-oriented and loyal to her friends. Onstage, she wore sexy clothes and flirted with the audience. In fact, people who knew Selena were surprised at what she would do on stage.

"When I'm onstage, I'm singing and I do things I (otherwise) wouldn't do," Selena told a reporter. "I'm more myself offstage. Not that I'm shy, but nervous and insecure about myself."

Offstage, Selena wanted to be a good role model for young people. She especially wanted to be a role model for Hispanic young people and help them through difficult times. "I see a lot of things going on these days that didn't when I was growing up," she said. She added that she wished someone would have taken the time to talk to her when she was young.

Selena often visited schools to talk to the students about the importance of an education. She also told them it was important to leave drugs alone. She helped out with the D.A.R.E. (Drug Abuse Resistance Education) program. She planned a fundraising concert to help people with AIDS (Acquired Immune Deficiency Syndrome).

"She was a very loving person," her father said. "She cared for people. She was concerned about so many issues in the Hispanic community, education, drugs, AIDS. She was just so busy."

Many nonprofit organizations contacted Selena about helping them. They knew she was one of the few entertainers who would donate her time and talents.

For-profit companies also talked to Selena. Coca-Cola hired Selena to be a spokesperson for their products when she was just seventeen. Selena also agreed to endorse a hair care company's products if they produced an educational video for students. They agreed and the video featuring Selena premiered at a middle school in Corpus Christi. Even as Selena encouraged other young people to get an education,

Selena attending one of the many charity benefits she was involved in.

she knew it would be hard to continue her own. She decided to earn a college degree the same way she had earned her diploma — through a correspondence program. She enrolled in business courses she could study while on the road doing concerts. "I thought I would get my degree (in fashion) design, because that fascinated me," she said. "But I feel I'll be of more service to my employees, my husband and my family if I know more about business."

FASHIONING A LIFE OFFSTAGE

Selena had always loved fashion design, even as a young girl. She decided her interest in fashion would help balance her life. She formed a company called Selena, Etc. She hoped her business would give her a rest from her celebrity life.

In 1993, she began designing and manufacturing her own line of clothing. She sold her clothing from two boutiques. When it came time to hire someone to manage the boutiques, Selena turned to fan club president Yolanda Saldivar.

Selena's new business added many demands to her schedule. Not only did she continue to design her clothing line, she also helped promote it. Photo shoots and fashion shows kept her busy between concerts. At the same time, the Selena Fan Club attracted more members.

Selena's businesses were making her and her family wealthy. The magazine *Hispanic Business* reported the singer earned $5 million in 1993 and 1994. It made her one of the top 20 wealthiest Hispanic entertainers in the world. It also made her the first Tejano artist ever to make that list.

Despite her many businesses and endorsements, Selena's records still made her the most money. Her "Selena Live!" earned the singer the music world's highest honor in 1993 — a Grammy Award for the best Mexican-American performance.

A few months later, Selena shared the spotlight with singer Jon Secada at the Latin Music Awards in Miami, Florida. Selena was named female artist of the year in the regional Mexican music category. She also won song of the year and album of the year.

Not only was Selena a Grammy-winning recording star, she owned clothing boutiques.

Selena's music was even more popular in Mexico. By fall 1994, her new album "Amor Prohibido" ("Forbidden Love") was selling two thousand copies a day in Mexico. That same year she won a small part in a new movie, *Don Juan DeMarco*. The movie starred Marlon Brando and Johnny Depp. The year 1994 also saw Selena y Los Dinos appear for the first time in New York, Los Angeles, Argentina and Puerto Rico.

CROSSING OVER TO POP

In 1995, Selena earned a second Grammy Award nomination. As she had in years past, she also swept the Tejano Music Awards. This time she received six awards, including top female vocalist. It was the eighth time she had received that honor.

Yet Selena's mind was on more than Tejano music. She was getting closer and closer to recording an album in English. Unlike her other albums, this one would not feature the Tejano sound.

Selena hoped to gain new fans with her English album. She wanted to be like Gloria Estefan. Estefan is a Cuban-American who began singing Latin music in Spanish. Later, she crossed over into popular music.

Selena turned to her brother, A.B., for help. A.B. had written many of the songs that propelled Selena y Los Dinos to stardom. Selena hoped he could produce her English album. By March 1995, Selena had recorded four tracks for the English album.

The record company was to release the English album in the summer of 1995. Selena also was working with A.B. on a Tejano album for a 1995 release. With two albums in the works, Selena had no extra time. That was the way she wanted it.

"A person should never be satisfied with what they've accomplished," she said. "Better to try than not to try at all."

Selena earned a second Grammy Award nomination in 1995.

SHADOW ON A BRIGHT HORIZON

Early in 1995, Selena and her family became concerned about the Selena Fan Club finances. Selena's friend Yolanda still handled the club.

"We started to get a lot of mail and a lot of phone calls from people," recalls her father, Abraham. "They were sending in checks and money and they never received the items that were supposed to be shipped, like T-shirts and cassettes. Yet she (Saldivar) was running the checks through the bank."

In March 1995, the Quintanilla family talked to Yolanda about the problem. Abraham remembered Yolanda didn't appear upset, and offered explanations. Selena decided to look for more evidence of wrongdoing. If she found it, she would fire Yolanda from her duties.

On March 30, Yolanda talked to Abraham. She promised to give the family the fan club and boutique business papers. That evening, Selena and her husband met Yolanda at her

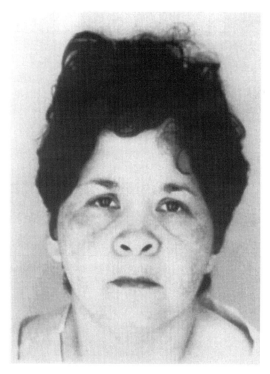

Yolanda Saldivar's police mug shot after she was booked for killing Selena.

motel to pick up the papers. When they got home, they realized some papers were missing.

The next day was Friday. Selena had a recording session scheduled that morning at 10:00. She skipped the session and went to Yolanda's motel room. Police believe she intended to fire Yolanda that morning. Regardless of what Selena wanted to do, she never made it to her recording session.

Police reports say Selena went to Yolanda's motel room shortly before noon. Witnesses said the two women argued. Then they heard a gunshot. Selena was shot once in the back of her right shoulder as she walked away. She staggered down a walkway and around a corner. The motel manager saw her and helped her inside.

An ambulance took Selena to Memorial Medical Center in Corpus Christi. She died there an hour later. Doctors said she had lost too much blood from the bullet wound.

TOO SOON, THE END

Back at the motel, police found Yolanda in her pickup truck holding a gun to her head. She stayed there for nine and a half hours. She threatened to kill herself. Finally, she surrendered to police, who took her to jail. Later she confessed to the shooting.

The Hispanic community was in shock as news of Selena's death spread. People could not believe the Queen of Tejano was dead. Fans immediately paid tribute to their fallen star.

Tens of thousands of fans came from around the United States and Mexico to Selena's middle-class brick home. They left flowers, stuffed animals, notes and balloons. Many left white roses, Selena's favorite flower. Some had signs saying "We love you, Selena." Throughout Corpus Christi, Selena's fans showed their respect. They drove with their headlights on. They cried and wrote poems. And they played her music.

When Selena died, her newest album was number four on the popular chart of Latin music. Her older, Grammy-winning album also jumped from 12,000 to 28,000 albums sold per week .

Many stores sold out of Selena albums within hours of the news of the singer's death. Tearful fans asked for something—anything—of Selena.

On Sunday, April 2, Selena's family held a public visitation. More than 50,000 fans silently filed by Selena's closed casket. They ranged in age from the very young to the very old. Many cried and prayed. Late in the day, the family opened the casket. Fans got one last look at their star. The family opened the casket to end a rumor that Selena's body was not inside.

April 2 would have been Selena's third wedding anniversary.

A TEARFUL FAREWELL

Selena's family held her funeral on Monday, April 3. She was buried in the same purple dress she wore when she won her Grammy Award. People at the service heaped 8,000 white roses on her grave.

Only family members and close friends attended the burial. Thousands of other fans waited outside the cemetery hoping to catch one last glimpse of Selena. They also hoped to see the famous Tejano musicians who had come to the funeral.

Family and friends listen during Selena's funeral sevices, April 3, 1995.

On the day of her funeral, the local newspaper printed notes from her fans. One read, "Selena will be remembered as a beautiful, talented young lady. She will always be in our hearts and will never be forgotten. But most of all she will be remembered as a young lady who took time out for children."

A Hispanic leader summed up the loss of Selena as a role model. "She was particularly valuable in the Hispanic community because we don't have many role models. She was an achiever and worked very hard at what she did. She taught people that hard work pays."

On Sunday, April 16, 1995, Selena would have been twenty-four years old. In her honor, Texas Governor George W. Bush declared the day "Selena Day" throughout the state. He praised Selena's determination and family devotion. He thanked her for all she had done for the community.

The world will never know how far Selena could have gone. She will live on through her music and her spirit. Already, her hometown leaders are planning a Selena Memorial. Meanwhile, the world of Tejano is hoping another star will spread this special music beyond the Hispanic world.

Perhaps Selena's greatest gift can be seen in the words of one admirer. "I will remember her by being kind to others, because that is what she taught me."

The world will never know how far Selena could have gone.

GLOSSARY

Boutique — a fashionable specialty store.

Correspondence course — a way of attending school through the mail.

Gigs — a band's engagement to play somewhere.

Grammy — a special award given to music industry people.

Latin — having to do with the Spanish-speaking people of North America.

Nonprofit — a business that is run for reasons other than to make money.

Phenomenal — incredible.

Polka — a lively type of dance music from Europe.

Soprano — the highest singing voice.

Visitation — the time before a funeral when people can pay their respects to someone who died.